THE USBORNE YOUNG SCIENTIST
TRAINS

Contents

Credits

Written by Jonathan Rutland and Margaret Stephens
Art and editorial direction David Jefferis
Editorial revision Margaret Stephens
Text editor Eliot Humberstone
Design Iain Ashman and John Jamieson
Design revision Robert Walster
Illustrators Malcolm English, John Hutchinson, Frank
Kennard, Michael Roffe, Robert Walster, Sean
Wilkinson, John Barker, Hans Wiborg-Jenssen, Abdul
Aziz Khan, Keith Talbot

This edition published 1991
Based on The Young Engineers Book of Supertrains,
published 1978.

Acknowledgements

National Railway Museum in York
Rail Magazine
SNCF
British Rail
German Railways
Japan Rail
Canadian National Railways
Airfix Products Ltd
Beatties of London Ltd
Dowty Hydraulic Units Ltd
Energy Equipment Co. Ltd
Airfix Products Ltd

Usborne Publishing Ltd
Usborne House
83-85 Saffron Hill
London EC1N 8RT

Printed in Belgium

Introduction

This book is full of amazing trains. As you turn the pages you will find fast trains, powerful trains, slow trains and astonishing trains. You will also discover that each train has a personality all of its own, whether this means it flies above the track without touching the rails, or has long legs which go under water.

There are tunnels, bridges, tracks and freight yards to read about too. Where is the longest tunnel in the world? Which bridge has the longest steel arch span? How do freight containers load onto rail wagons?

All the facts are explained very simply and there are experiments to help you really understand how things work. There is even a step-by-step guide to how a steam locomotive works, and a cutaway picture of the latest high-speed, magnetic levitation train.

This book will really show you how exciting and intriguing the world of trains can be.

Introducing the steam locomotive

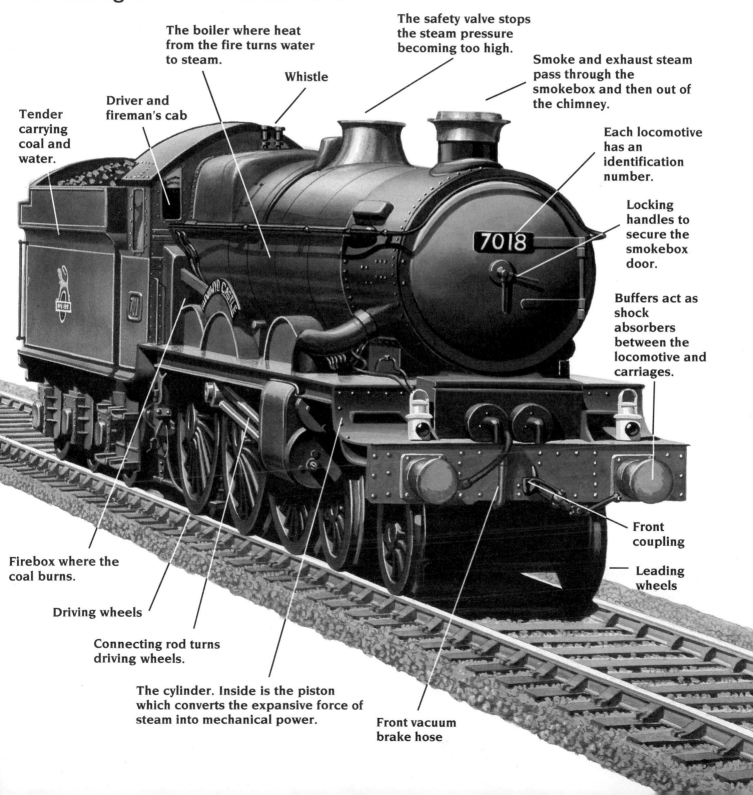

The boiler where heat from the fire turns water to steam.

The safety valve stops the steam pressure becoming too high.

Whistle

Smoke and exhaust steam pass through the smokebox and then out of the chimney.

Driver and fireman's cab

Tender carrying coal and water.

Each locomotive has an identification number.

7018

Locking handles to secure the smokebox door.

Buffers act as shock absorbers between the locomotive and carriages.

Firebox where the coal burns.

Driving wheels

Connecting rod turns driving wheels.

The cylinder. Inside is the piston which converts the expansive force of steam into mechanical power.

Front vacuum brake hose

Front coupling

Leading wheels

The magic of trains

The four famous trains shown here come from Great Britain, France and the USA. Great Britain and the USA were the first to develop modern railways. But nowadays France is one of the leading countries in railway technology and while other countries are running down their railways and closing routes, France is laying new track and building the fastest trains in the world.

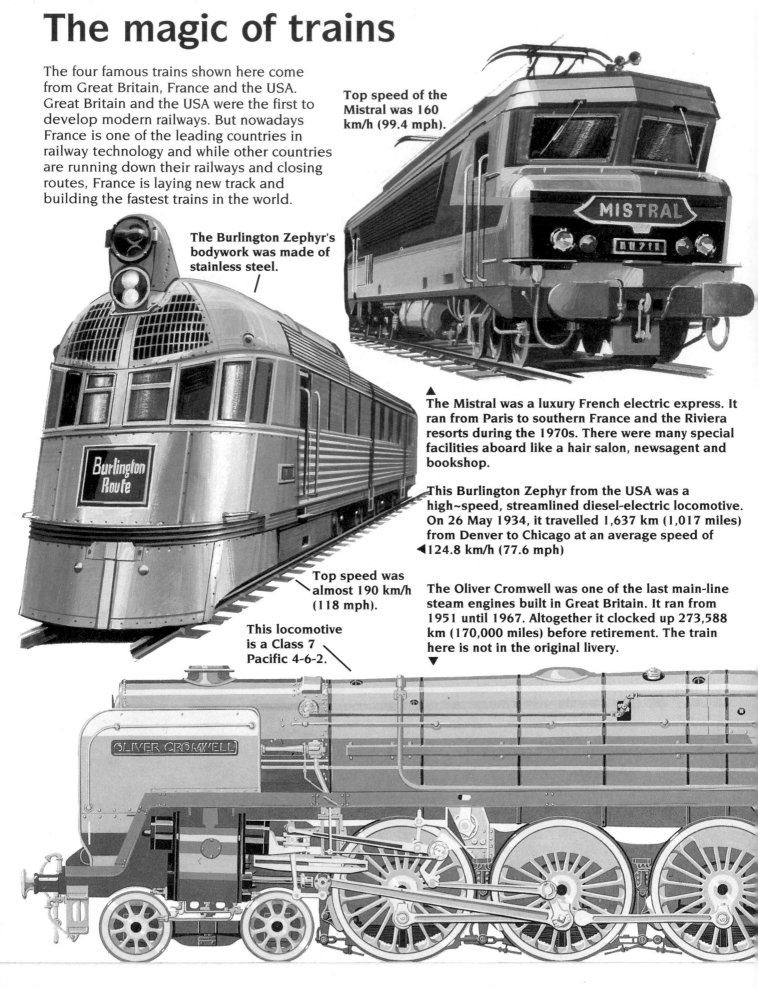

Top speed of the Mistral was 160 km/h (99.4 mph).

The Burlington Zephyr's bodywork was made of stainless steel.

The Mistral was a luxury French electric express. It ran from Paris to southern France and the Riviera resorts during the 1970s. There were many special facilities aboard like a hair salon, newsagent and bookshop.

This Burlington Zephyr from the USA was a high~speed, streamlined diesel-electric locomotive. On 26 May 1934, it travelled 1,637 km (1,017 miles) from Denver to Chicago at an average speed of ◀124.8 km/h (77.6 mph)

Top speed was almost 190 km/h (118 mph).

This locomotive is a Class 7 Pacific 4-6-2.

The Oliver Cromwell was one of the last main-line steam engines built in Great Britain. It ran from 1951 until 1967. Altogether it clocked up 273,588 km (170,000 miles) before retirement. The train here is not in the original livery.
▼

The first railway to provide meals on a train was the Baltimore and Ohio Railroad, USA, in 1853.

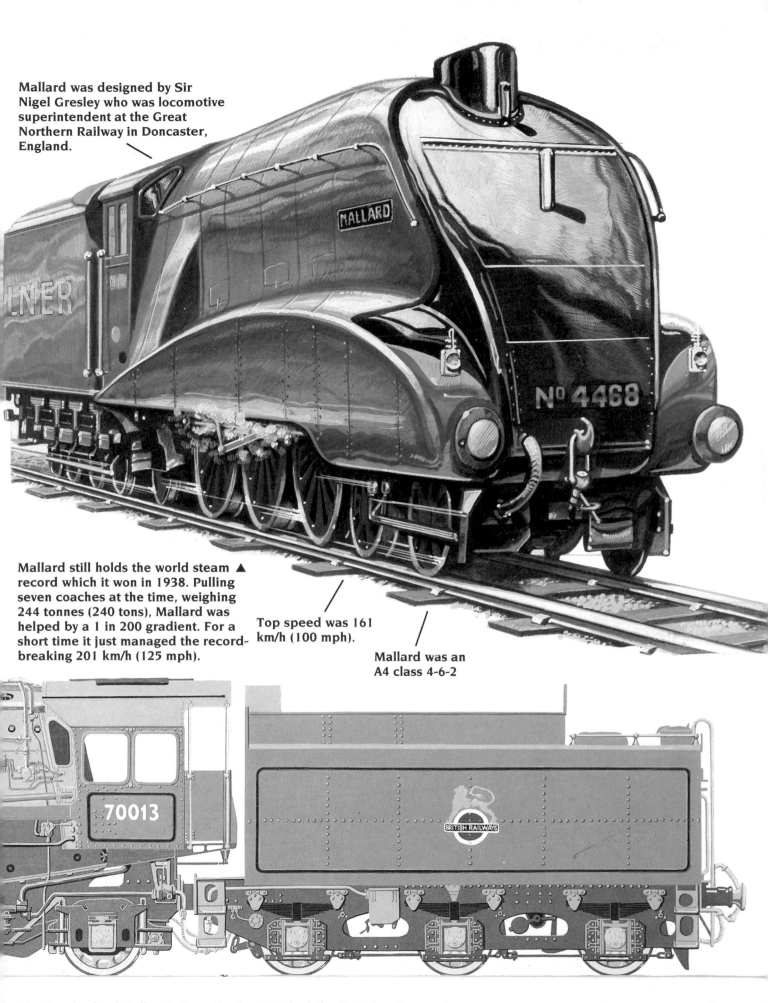

Mallard was designed by Sir Nigel Gresley who was locomotive superintendent at the Great Northern Railway in Doncaster, England.

Mallard still holds the world steam ▲ record which it won in 1938. Pulling seven coaches at the time, weighing 244 tonnes (240 tons), Mallard was helped by a 1 in 200 gradient. For a short time it just managed the record-breaking 201 km/h (125 mph).

Top speed was 161 km/h (100 mph).

Mallard was an A4 class 4-6-2

The Cumberland Valley Railroad in the USA had the first sleeping carriages.

The first trains

About 3,000 years ago, the Ancient Greeks made grooves in stone paths to guide wagon wheels. These wagonways were the simple forerunners of the track you now find in modern railways. Nearly 2,500 years later, wooden rails were being used for mine railways. Coal wagons had wooden wheels, with flanges (rims to keep them on the rails). Horses walked between the rails pulling the wagons along the track. Later some metal rails were flanged too, in an "L" shape.

Much later, metal was laid over the wooden rails to save them from wear and tear. Then by 1800, metal rails were invented. Today's rails are made of steel.

The power of steam has been known for more than 2,000 years, but the first steam engine was only invented in 1712. It pumped water out of flooded mines. In 1804, Richard Trevithick of Cornwall in England built a steam locomotive that pulled passengers and freight at 8 km/h (5 mph). Many engineers all over the world then began to design their own steam locomotives. One of the most famous of these early railway engineers was Robert Stephenson, who designed and built many trains and railway bridges.

The Best Friend of Charleston, 1830 ▶

This locomotive ran on the first regular train service in the USA. Once its boiler exploded when the fireman tied down the steam valve because the noise of escaping steam was annoying him.

This oddity, a sailing rail car, ran on America's Baltimore and Ohio Railroad in 1830. It was a success only when the wind blew the right way. One day the sailing master forgot to brake at the end of the line, and crashed into a bank.

▲ The Rocket, 1829

In 1829 a competition was held to find the most reliable locomotive for the new Liverpool to Manchester Railway. There was a £500 prize. George Stephenson and his son Robert, who was 26 years old, entered Rocket. Robert had in fact done most of the design work on Rocket. Their locomotive won easily. It made 20 trips of 2.8 km (1.7 miles) each, at an average speed of 20 km/h (12.4 mph), pulling wagons weighing 13.2 tonnes (13 tons).

Der Adler, 1835 ▶

This locomotive was used on the first German railway, from Nuremberg to Fürth. Der Adler was built by Robert Stephenson's company, at Newcastle-Upon-Tyne

One of Rocket's rivals in the 1829 competition was powered by two horses turning a treadmill.

Rolling on rails

A loaded wagon rolling along level track at 100 km/h (62 mph) can freewheel for at least 8 km (5 miles) before stopping. On a road, a lorry of the same weight stops after only 1.5 km (nearly one mile). Smooth metal wheels roll much more easily on smooth metal rails than rubber tyres do on roads. This is why locomotives can haul such enormous loads. The first wheels and rails were wood, but modern metal wheels and rails mean trains can go faster and the track is more hard wearing.

You can see the difference a smooth surface makes with this experiment. Collect together a model train wagon, some track, plasticine, cotton thread and a towel.

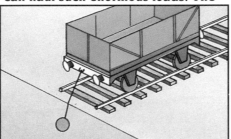

Put the model wagon on some track at the edge of a table. Tie the wagon's coupling to 40 cm (16 in) of cotton thread. Fix a ball of plasticine to the other end of the thread. Hang the plasticine ball over the table and adjust the weight so it just starts the wagon rolling.

Now place the towel on the table and smooth it down flat. Take the wagon off the rails and put it on the towel. Try again to find the weight of plasticine that starts the wagon rolling. You will discover that it does not move unless you use a much bigger piece of plasticine.

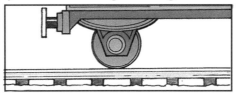

This is a metal wheel on a metal rail. As the wheel turns it meets little resistance, as both the rail and wheel are smooth. This means it needs less weight to pull it along.

When a wheel meets the towel's rough surface, resistance is much greater, so the wagon needs a heavier weight to pull it. This resistance is called friction.

in England. It had three pairs of wheels, one more than Rocket, which meant it could carry a large boiler.

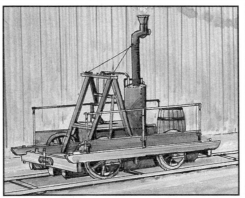

The first steam locomotive on the Baltimore and Ohio Railroad in the USA was a strange looking contraption called Tom Thumb. It was built in 1829 but first ran in 1930. The boiler was vertical and the locomotive had one cylinder.

Some inventors came up with the idea of steam road carriages that ran without rails. This one was built in 1832. It needed someone hanging on the back to feed the fire with coal. The design was very similar to the horse-pulled coaches of those times.

The first passenger railway in the world started in Wales in 1807. Horses pulled the wagons.

Steam power

From Rocket to the present day, the basic design of steam engines has remained the same. The remarkably simple principles of steam power can be seen in this cutaway picture of a classic American locomotive.

About 20,000 of these locos were built between 1840 and 1890, and the 4-4-0 wheel code is known as an American. The engines usually burned wood because only a few coal mines were operating at the time. Just 4% of the fire's heat was used to pull the wheels. Most of the heat went up the chimney, which was designed to catch sparks from the burning wood. The large oil lamp on the front of the locomotive helped the driver to see animals on the track at night.

Another hazard at night was the danger of ambush, and the light's strong beam was essential to spot criminals waiting by the track. As cows could derail a train, the wide cowcatcher on the front was designed to sweep away animals straying onto the track.

Pulling a 150 tonne (147.6 ton) train at 65 km/h (40.4 mph), the firebox used 45 kg of wood per 1 km (163 lbs per mile).

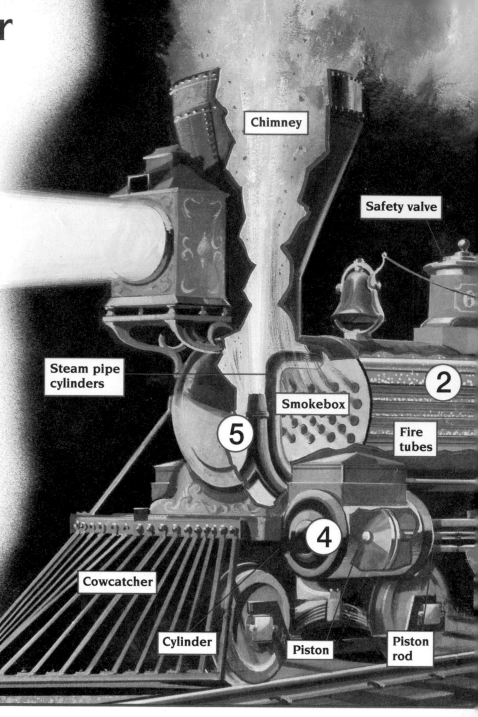

Chimney

Safety valve

Steam pipe cylinders

Smokebox

Fire tubes

5

2

4

Cowcatcher

Cylinder

Piston

Piston rod

Wheel codes

A steam locomotive's wheel code shows how many wheels it has and what job they do. The first figure in the code gives the number of leading wheels, the second the driving wheels, and the third the trailing wheels.

This system is known as the Whyte notation because it was invented by railroad official Frederick Whyte in the USA, in 1900.

2-6-0
Mogul

2-6-2
Prairie

2-6-4
Adriatic

2-8-0
Consolidation

2-8-2
Mikado

2-10-0
Decapod

2-10-2
Santa Fé

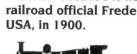
4-4-2
Atlantic

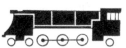
4-6-2
Pacific

4-6-4
Hudson

4-8-2
Mountain

4-8-4
Northern

1 The firebox

The firebox contains the engine's coal or wood fire. The heat from the firebox is used to boil water in the boiler, which creates steam.

2 The boiler

The boiler is really a large metal barrel of water. Inside are lots of hollow fire tubes heated by hot air coming from the firebox. As the water in the boiler come in contact with the tubes it begins to boil. Steam is generated by the boiling water and collects in the dome.

3 The dome

As steam collects in the dome, pressure begins to build up. When the pressure is high enough, the driver opens the regulator valve by working a regulator handle in his cab. Steam then passes through the steam pipes and rushes into the cylinders. These are mounted on each side of the locomotive over the bogie with the leading wheels.

③

①

Tender

Crank

Connecting rod

4 The cylinder

Slide valve

Piston

Steam inlet

Steam outlet

Inside each cylinder is a piston. Steam (orange) is fed into the cylinder first on one side of the piston and then on the other, controlled by the slide valve. In this way the piston is pushed backwards and forwards. This action, linked through a connecting rod and crank, turns the driving wheels. At the end of each piston stroke, exhausted steam escapes through the blastpipe and out of the chimney. Each puff of a steam train is made by a rush of steam up the blastpipe.

5 The blastpipe

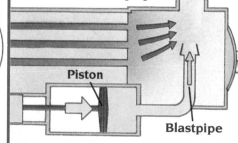

Piston

Blastpipe

When exhaust steam from the cylinder is forced up the blastpipe, this draws hot air from the firebox along the fire tubes which heat up the water. At the same time, a draught is created in the firebox, which makes the fire burn well.

In Tasmania, Australia, in 1836 people paid a shilling to ride in trucks pushed by convicts.

Modern locomotives

Passenger carriages

Diesel engine

Fuel tank

Modern trains rarely use steam to power their engines. Diesel and electricity have taken over as the two main sources of energy. Steam trains look splendid, but their engines are very wasteful. Only about 9% of the fire's energy is used to drive the wheels. Steam trains are very dirty and emit a lot of atmospheric pollution too.

Diesel and electric power are much more efficient. Overall, electric locomotives are more costly to run than diesel ones, because the installation of trackside equipment is high. So electric locos are only profitable on routes with lots of passengers.

Diesel power

This is British Rail's High Speed Train (HST). Top speed in service is 201 km/h (125 mph). The locomotives at either end of the train are diesel-electrics. This means that the power actually turning the wheels is electricity.

The engine burns diesel, which is pumped up from tanks beneath the locomotive. The power from the burning diesel then turns a generator which produces electricity. This electricity is passed to the traction motors which turn the driving wheels.

One of the problems with fast trains is braking within a safe distance. HSTs have disc brakes on all carriage and locomotive wheels.

Electric power

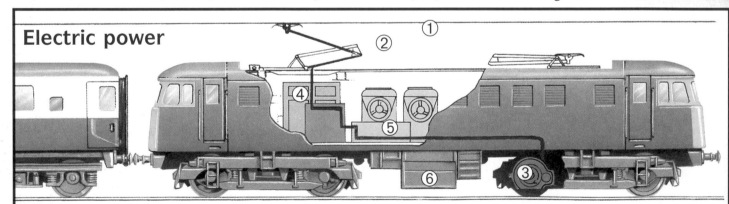

This British Rail locomotive, Class 85, runs on electricity. The power supply comes from overhead wires (1) and is fed into the engine by pantographs (2) which stretch up from the locomotive's roof. The pantographs press firmly against the wires, and can be lowered when necessary. A very high, mains current voltage is transmitted through the pantographs. As low voltage motors (3) are easier and cheaper to run than high voltage ones, the current is changed to low voltage by transformers (4) and a rectifier (5). Class 85s have batteries (6) which power the control circuits and lighting. The locomotive's roof panels are removable to allow the installation and taking out of equipment.

The first public electric railway ran near Berlin, Germany, in 1881. It carried 26 passengers on each journey.

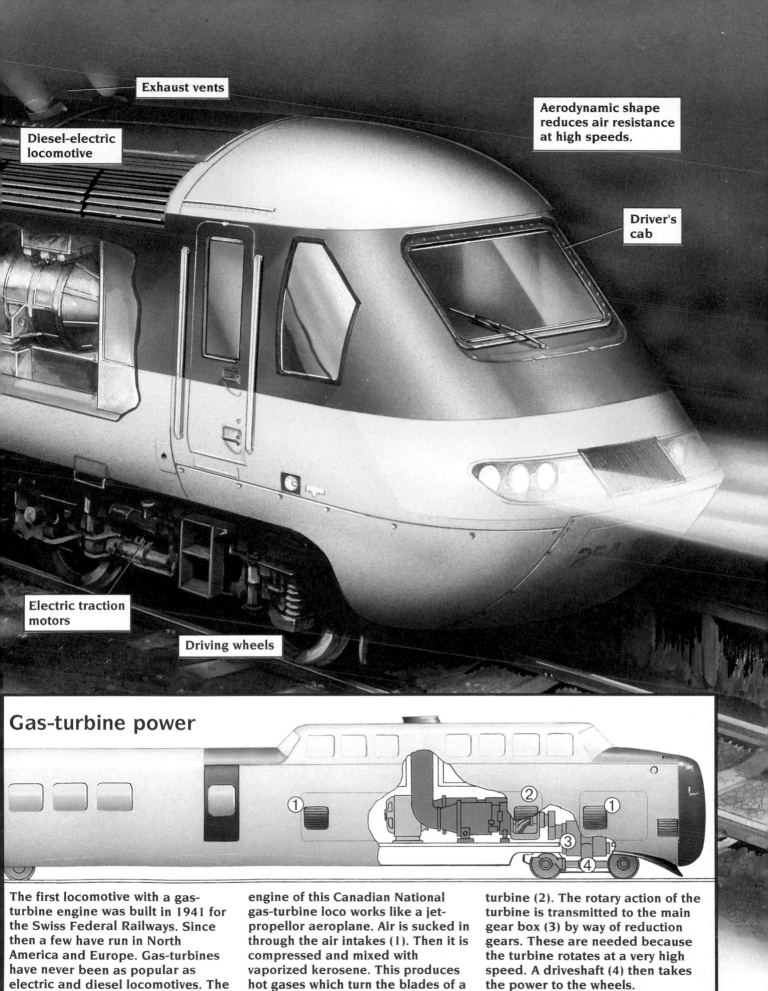

Exhaust vents

Diesel-electric locomotive

Aerodynamic shape reduces air resistance at high speeds.

Driver's cab

Electric traction motors

Driving wheels

Gas-turbine power

The first locomotive with a gas-turbine engine was built in 1941 for the Swiss Federal Railways. Since then a few have run in North America and Europe. Gas-turbines have never been as popular as electric and diesel locomotives. The engine of this Canadian National gas-turbine loco works like a jet-propellor aeroplane. Air is sucked in through the air intakes (1). Then it is compressed and mixed with vaporized kerosene. This produces hot gases which turn the blades of a turbine (2). The rotary action of the turbine is transmitted to the main gear box (3) by way of reduction gears. These are needed because the turbine rotates at a very high speed. A driveshaft (4) then takes the power to the wheels.

Between 1940 and 1967, the proportion of diesel pulled trains in the USA rose from under 1% to 99%.

Light rail transit - monorails

Light rail transit systems carry large numbers of passengers on short journeys, in the quickest possible time. They are electrically operated and usually found in cities where they help ease congestion on busy roads. Modern automatic systems can carry 50,000 passengers an hour. Trams, tubes and monorails are all examples of light rail transit. Monorails can look ugly built over city streets, and they make a lot of noise, but they are cheap to build. The train either runs on top of the rail, or it hangs from beneath. The first passenger monorail was built in 1876.

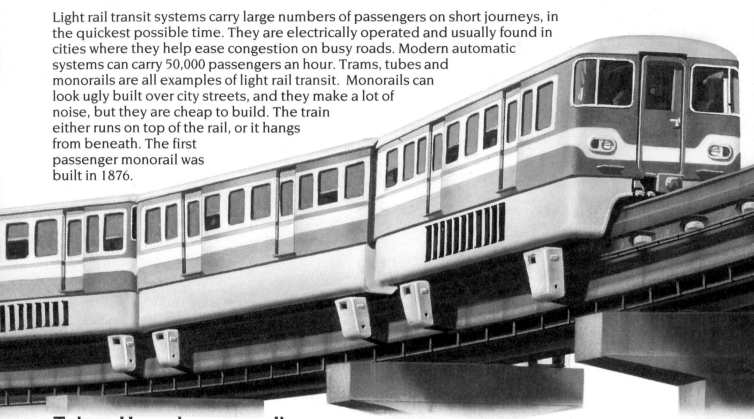

Tokyo-Haneda monorail

The Tokyo-Haneda monorail runs 13.1 km (8.1 miles) between Tokyo and the Haneda international airport, in 15 minutes. The train straddles a concrete beam. This method is known as the Hitachi-Alweg system. The track stands on concrete pylons which elevate it above the countryside. The train has two running wheels which propel it along the track. There are guide and stabilizing wheels too, that grip the side of the track, to keep the train balanced and secure.

Wuppertal Schwebebahn

The Wuppertal Schwebebahn is a suspended, cranked-arm type monorail. Most of the track runs over the Wupper River in Germany. From 1901 to 1960 it carried 1,000 million passengers. This monorail has a system where sections of movable track switch position, so trains can turn for the return journey.

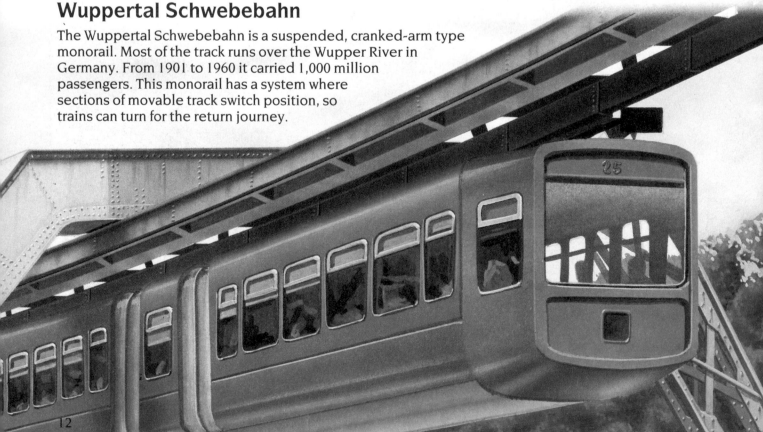

Light rail transit - trams and tubes

Underground railways, or tubes, are the most common type of light rail transit. Many cities throughout the world have a tube. In Paris it is called the metro and in New York, the subway. Trams have carriages that look more like buses than trains, and they run on rails which can be laid on roads, or have their own special track.

Four light rail systems

1 The Hitachi-Alweg monorail
2 The cranked-arm type monorail
3 Tram
4 Tube in underground tunnel

①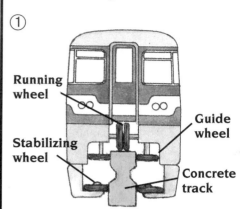

Running wheel
Guide wheel
Stabilizing wheel
Concrete track

②
Wheel running inside rail

Carriage hangs from track.

③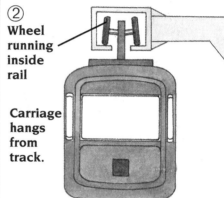

Pantograph

Rails in the road

④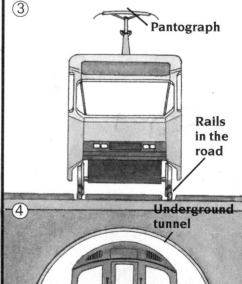

Underground tunnel

Melbourne tram

City 57
2001

▲ The tram above runs in the city of Melbourne in Australia, which has the largest system in the southern hemisphere. The city has converted under-used railways to tramways.

The London Underground below carries 815 million passengers a year. All the routes put together total 408 km (253.5 miles). 167 km (104 miles) of this is below ground. ▼

London underground train

MORDEN
053

Ups and downs

Railway engineers are faced with many problems when they lay track. Locomotives run best on level straight track. So how do they build track across a river or steep ravine? How can they avoid hills? How can they avoid bends, which slow a train down?

Sometimes track can be laid over a different route to avoid the problem. If this is impossible viaducts or bridges are built to carry trains over valleys and rivers, and cuttings are made in hills to straighten out bends. Tunnels are built too, through hills and under rivers.

Other ways of overcoming the problems of steep gradients are to increase the grip of wheels by fitting gears, dropping sand on rails, or using a rack and pinion system. Zig-zag track reduces the gradient in steep mountainous areas, but increases the travelling distance and running costs as trains travel backwards and forwards up the zig-zags. Tunnels that loop, climbing gently through mountains, can solve these problems, but are costly to build.

To the right is a section of the Landwasser Viaduct in Switzerland. It is part of the Rhaetian Railway and has six masonry arches. The track is 65 m (213 ft) above ground.

The Channel Tunnel

When the Channel Tunnel opens between France and England in 1993, it will be the second longest tunnel in the world at 49.4 km (30.7 miles). (For the longest see page 31.) The tunnel will also be about 100 m (328 ft) below sea level.

There will be two rail tunnels at 7.6 m (24 ft 11 in) in diameter, and one service tunnel at 4.8 m (15 ft 10 in) in diameter. Three types of train will run through it, a tunnel shuttle, a high-speed passenger train and a freight train.

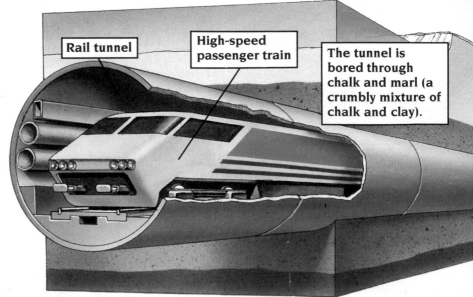

Rail tunnel

High-speed passenger train

The tunnel is bored through chalk and marl (a crumbly mixture of chalk and clay).

The world's longest brick viaduct is the London-Greenwich. It is about 6,000 m (19,000 ft) long, with 878 arches.

Sydney Harbour Bridge

Steel arch span

North shore

South shore

Sydney Harbour is very deep.

Tower supporting bridge.

Sydney Harbour Bridge in Australia stretches 1,149 m (3,770 ft) from the north to the south shore. It is a vital rail and road link between the two, with an eight-lane road, two rail tracks and a footpath. The famous steel arch span is the longest in the world at 503 m (1,650 ft). There were engineering problems of deep harbour water and the absence of any natural supports, like an island. Two massive towers, faced with granite, were built on both shores to support the bridge.

Getting it straight

A train uses lots of energy to build up speed. Once it has done so, little power is needed to keep it rolling on a straight and level track. Climbing gradients uses up much more power, and wheels slip easily on smooth metal. Laying track around hills is costly because it takes longer and uses up more materials. Track can be laid as straight and level as possible by cuttings, bridges, viaducts and tunnels.

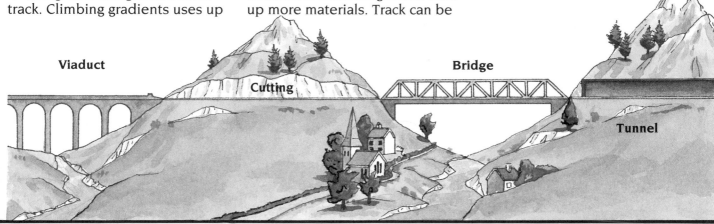

Viaduct

Cutting

Bridge

Tunnel

Hillclimbers

The Pilatus line in Switzerland is the world's steepest railway. To stop wheels slipping it has a rack and pinion drive. Toothed wheels (the pinions) turn in a toothed rail (the rack) to pull the train uphill.

Another way to stop wheels slipping on hills is by using gears. These help the engine turn the wheels more slowly. This increases their grip. The geared locomotive here hauled timber in America.

Many steam locomotives had a device for pouring sand on the rails in front of the driving wheels to improve grip. The Indian train here carried men on the front to sprinkle sand on the rails.

Rails and tracks

Baseplate

Fishplate joins rails together.

Wood or concrete sleepers

Spike - can be one of several designs

Steel T-rail

The sleepers are laid on ballast which is usually made of broken stone like granite.

Rails are vital to guide trains along a route. Concrete, steel or wood sleepers rest on stony ballast.

T-shaped steel rails are laid on the sleepers. Most rails are continuously welded, but fishplates sometimes still join different sections. In hot lands, continuously welded rail is stretched before laying, so it does not buckle by expanding in high temperatures.

The distance between rails is a gauge. A standard gauge of 1.435 m (4 ft 8½ in) is the most common worldwide. George Stephenson developed this gauge, basing it on the track mostly used for horse-pulled coal wagons.

Multi-gauge track

Some countries have several different gauges. This means loads have to be transferred from one train to another where gauges change. The diagram below shows the multi-gauge track of South Australia which handles three different sized trains, each using separate pairs of rails.

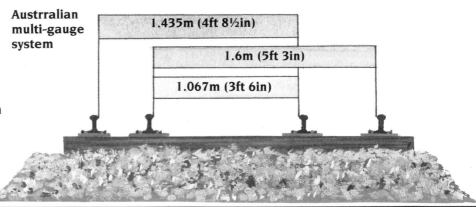

Austrralian multi-gauge system

1.435m (4ft 8½in)

1.6m (5ft 3in)

1.067m (3ft 6in)

Locomotive weight distribution

High-speed locomotives depend on their design and the quality of track for safety. As locomotives take sharp bends, they tend to be thrown outwards, which can be very dangerous. To counteract this, most of their weight is distributed low down near the base of the engine, because the higher their weight, the more chance there is of them tipping over.

A good way of testing this is to run a model train too fast. The experiment here shows the effect of different weight distribution.

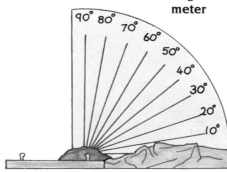

Angle meter

First make this meter to show the angle at which the train overbalances. Use stiff cardboard and draw angles from 0 to 90 like in the picture above. Prop up the meter with plasticine.

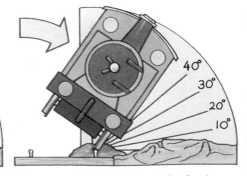

Use a model train, or a block of wood, and gradually tip it. When it starts to overbalance, note the angle on the meter. If you use a model train have a piece of soft cloth under it in case it falls.

Different trains for different gauges

Hiawatha Express

North Star

Romney, Hythe and Dymchurch locomotive

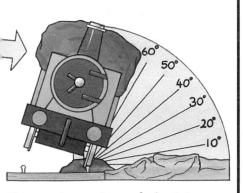

60°
50°
40°
30°
20°
10°

Now wedge a piece of plasticine on top of the train. Start tipping it again and you will notice that it overbalances more quickly at a smaller angle. A higher distribution of weight has made it less stable.

The British steam locomotive to the left above was the Great Western Railway's North Star. From 1838 to 1892 it ran on the widest gauge in railway history - 2.134 m (7 ft).

To the right of this train is the tiny locomotive that runs on the Romney, Hythe and Dymchurch Railway in England. This train runs on a gauge of 3.81 cm (1 ft 3 in).

The railway holds the rail speed record for a narrow gauge. A locomotive with 14 coaches ran without stopping for 43.2 km (26.8 mph) with a time of 73 mins 22 secs, and at an average speed of 35.4 km/h (22 mph), in 1982.

The huge locomotive above and below is an Atlantic with a 4-4-2 wheelcode. Atlantics were built in the USA between 1935 and 1937. This oil-fired loco ran on standard gauge and pulled the Hiawatha Express at a speed of 161 km/h (100 mph). Top speeds reached were up to 193 km/h (120 mph). Only four of these streamlined locomotives were ever built.

On standard gauge track in Britain, each kilometre of track weighs 111 tonnes (each mile weighs 151 tons).

Technology takes over

Railways need the latest computer and engineering technology so that trains can compete with other modern transport like planes and cars. New inventions can make railways faster and also make them more convenient and comfortable.

Some trains now have computers instead of drivers. The Docklands Light Railway in London, shown on the right, has driverless trains. A computer on board knows exactly where to coast, accelerate and brake between stations.

If there are problems, an operator in the control centre can take over by transmitting messages to the train.

By operating a push button in the Docklands Light Railway control room, a supervisor can stop a train instantly in an emergency.

BART

BART stands for the Bay Area Rapid Transit system, which operates in San Francisco and Oakland on the west coast of the USA. The line runs above, on, and under the ground as it threads its way through towns and suburbs. The BART carriages are made of lightweight aluminium alloy. Using advanced computer technology, everything is completely automated. Passengers put their money into automatic fare collection gates and enter the train through doors operated by computers.

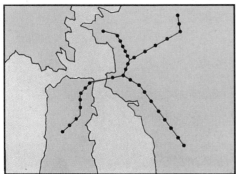

This map shows the 120 km (74.6 mile) long BART system. Part of it travels under the waters of San Francisco Bay. The 5.8 km (3.6 mile) underwater tunnel is made of pre-cast concrete sections.

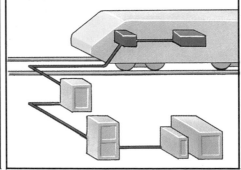

A computer in the control centre sends messages to a transmitter. The transmitter then passes these messages down wires on the track. A train's electronic sensors picks up the messages and feeds

them into its control box. A driver still sits in the cockpit, but the control box changes speeds and stops and starts the train. If anything goes wrong the driver or the controller can take over.

CATE

If you want to know which train to catch, then ring CATE (Computer Assisted Timetable Enquiries). All you do is phone and tell the computer operator where you want to go from, your destination, and the date and approximate time of your journey. Two seconds later the computer will have worked out the times and the best way to go. CATE will also tell you if your train has any food on board or a phone, and of course how much your ticket costs. These complex systems can operate on huge rail networks with thousands of stations, routes and trains.

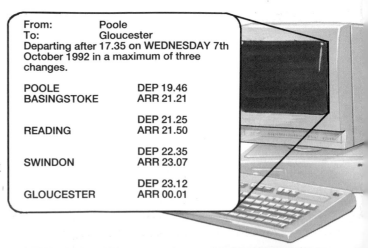

From: Poole
To: Gloucester
Departing after 17.35 on WEDNESDAY 7th October 1992 in a maximum of three changes.

POOLE	DEP 19.46
BASINGSTOKE	ARR 21.21
	DEP 21.25
READING	ARR 21.50
	DEP 22.35
SWINDON	ARR 23.07
	DEP 23.12
GLOUCESTER	ARR 00.01

British Rail - scientific research

British Rail has a special scientific research centre that invents and tests the latest railway technology. Seven hundred scientists and engineers work on projects there. One project is an electronic signalling system linking train drivers to control centres which supervise train traffic. Paved concrete track without sleepers and ballast is another invention. They can match paints by computer too (like the picture here), and have invented a special chemical formula to stop bridges corroding.

Canadian ATCS

Canadian National Railways have a way of guiding and controlling freight trains, called ATCS (Advanced Train Control Systems). At Jasper Station in Alberta, a train carrying 92 grain wagons begins a journey. As it gathers speed, underneath the train electronic sensors start scanning the track. They are looking for a transponder. When the sensors pass over a transponder, the transponder feeds a message through the sensor to the train's computer. This message is then transmitted by the train's aerial to a computer control centre. In this way the control centre always knows exactly where all their trains are and the speed at which they are travelling.

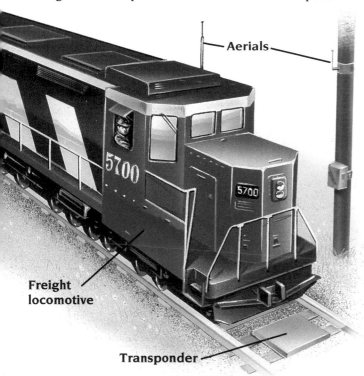

Aerials

5700

5700

Freight locomotive

Transponder

Computerized control

This computer in the driver's cab will tell the crew exactly where they are, how long the train is, and the train's speed. It keeps in constant contact with a computerized traffic control centre.

Computer and screen in driver's cab.

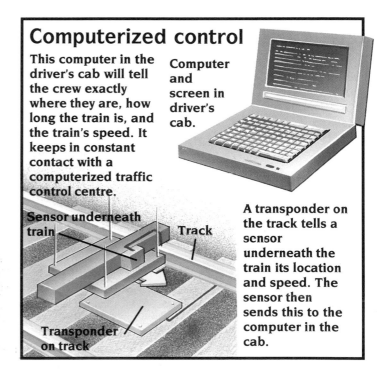

A transponder on the track tells a sensor underneath the train its location and speed. The sensor then sends this to the computer in the cab.

Sensor underneath train

Track

Transponder on track

TGV wind tunnel

This is a computer model of the French TGV in a wind tunnel. Wind tunnels test the flow of air around trains. Air can behave rather like water. An oar with the blade turned sideways is easy to pull through water. It is much harder when the wide flat part of the blade is pulled through water, as this creates more resistance. Resistance happens when trains travel through air too, and slows them down. It is important that fast trains are as aerodynamic as possible by being long and slender, like the TGV.

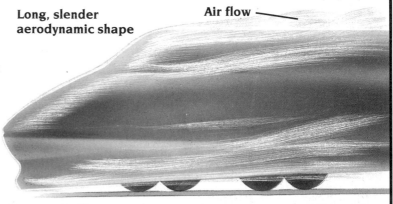

Long, slender aerodynamic shape

Air flow

If the crew of an ATCS train forget to brake in time, the computer in the cab will apply the brakes for them.

Maglev trains

Maglevs are trains of the future that will give passengers a smooth, silent ride. They operate on the principle of magnetic levitation, which means the trains are suspended above the track. As they never come in contact with the track there is less friction so they can go faster, and there is much less wear and tear which saves money on maintenance. Two types of maglev have been developed. The Japanese Linear Express operates in a guideway by magnetic repulsion and attraction, and the German Transrapid and the Birmingham maglev operate suspended over a track by attraction. The Birmingham maglev is in service now and the Japanese maglev starts in the year 2000.

Japanese Linear Express

MLB OOX1

Side magnet

The Japanese Linear Express

The Japanese Linear Express will probably be the fastest train in the world when it finally comes into service. Japan Rail promise that it will run at an average speed of 500 km/h (311 mph), with a top speed of almost 600 km/h (373 mph). One problem is the effect of the strong magnets, which can cause sickness among passengers.

Magnetic power

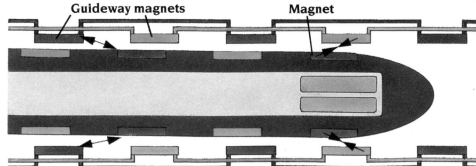

Guideway magnets

Magnet

Magnet   **Magnet**

Magnets

Levetation coil

The Linear Express runs in a guideway. As it gathers speed, magnets in its underside create an electrical current in coils in the guideway floor. These then become magnetic too and repel the train's

magnets, lifting it off the track by 10 cm (4 in), at 100 km/h (62 mph).

The train moves by magnets in the sides of the guideway and train. These have alternating north and south poles, controlled by computer.

The attraction and repulsion forces created propel the train. Repulsion forces act from the back and attraction forces act from the front, to push the train forward through the guideway.

The German Transrapid has a solid track mounted on pillars which elevates the train across the countryside.

Birmingham maglev

The British Birmingham maglev travels at about 53 km/h (34 mph), from the city's airport to its railway station. The track is T-shaped and the bottom of the train slots into the top flat bit of the "T". The part of the train beneath the track is attracted upwards by magnets on the underside of the track. This attraction pushes up the main body of the train above the track for a friction free ride. The German Transrapid also works on this principle, but is much faster.

Train lifted up by magnetic attraction.

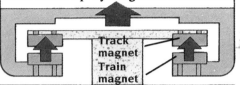

Track magnet
Train magnet

Aerodynamics

The Linear Express is aerodynamically designed to make it as streamlined as possible. It is a long pencil-shaped train with a pointed oval nose, built to achieve the highest speeds.

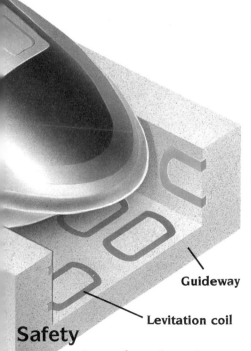

Guideway

Levitation coil

Safety

The attraction and repulsion forces of the side magnets also keep the Linear Express running safely in the centre of the guideway. If a train moves to one side, repulsion and attraction forces act to move the train back to the centre. This principle works even better at high speeds.

Maglev experiment

This simple experiment will show you how magnetic repulsion forces lift the Japanese Linear Express from the floor of its guideway.

Collect together two horseshoe magnets, two pieces of stiff cardboard and some strong glue.

The ends of each magnet are either a north or south pole. If two identical poles come together they repel. Two different poles will attract. Glue the ends of each magnet firmly to the centre of each piece of cardboard.

Pick up each piece of cardboard by its magnet. Slide one cardboard over the other. What happens when the magnets meet in the middle? Do they repel or attract? Try it again, but switch one piece of cardboard round. When the same poles meet the two pieces will repel each other and push apart. This is what happens when the maglev lifts up from the floor of its guideway.

Cardboard   Magnet

Glue

When north and south poles meet the pieces of cardboard will attract each other.

When the same poles meet the pieces of cardboard will repel each other.

Freight handling

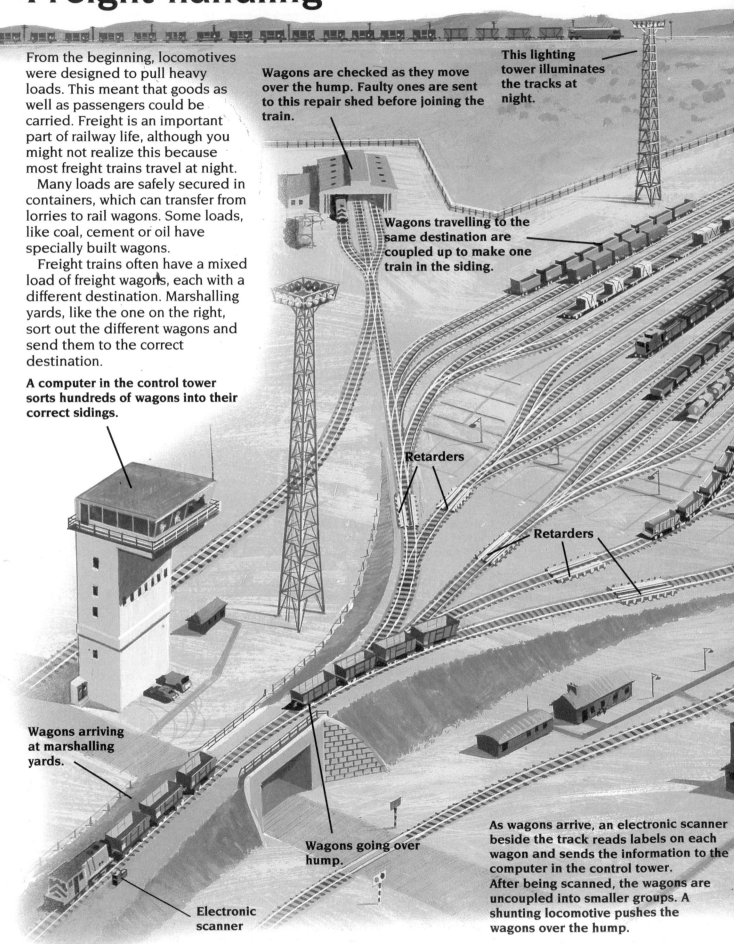

From the beginning, locomotives were designed to pull heavy loads. This meant that goods as well as passengers could be carried. Freight is an important part of railway life, although you might not realize this because most freight trains travel at night.

Many loads are safely secured in containers, which can transfer from lorries to rail wagons. Some loads, like coal, cement or oil have specially built wagons.

Freight trains often have a mixed load of freight wagons, each with a different destination. Marshalling yards, like the one on the right, sort out the different wagons and send them to the correct destination.

A computer in the control tower sorts hundreds of wagons into their correct sidings.

Wagons are checked as they move over the hump. Faulty ones are sent to this repair shed before joining the train.

This lighting tower illuminates the tracks at night.

Wagons travelling to the same destination are coupled up to make one train in the siding.

Retarders

Retarders

Wagons arriving at marshalling yards.

Wagons going over hump.

Electronic scanner

**As wagons arrive, an electronic scanner beside the track reads labels on each wagon and sends the information to the computer in the control tower.
After being scanned, the wagons are uncoupled into smaller groups. A shunting locomotive pushes the wagons over the hump.**

Freight carrying containers were first used as early as 1849 on the Camden and Amboy Railroad, USA.

A train leaves to join the main line.

As wagons roll downhill from the hump, the computer in the control tower operates points and retarders (see below) to send the wagons in the correct direction. This means each wagon rolls gently into the correct siding.

Transporting goods in containers

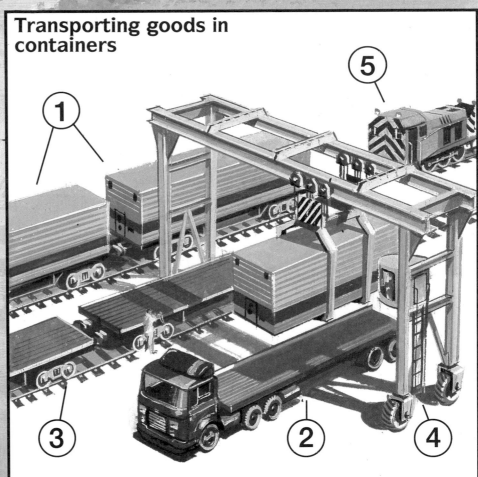

Containers 1 are like giant packing cases. Each container is a standard size that fits onto container lorries 2, rail wagons 3, and into the grabs of container cranes 4. Packed containers are sent by road to a road-rail container terminal. There they are transferred to a rail wagon by the crane. A shunting locomotive 5 then takes the wagon off to join a container train. Containers arriving at docks after a sea journey are loaded straight onto wagons.

Slowing down wagons

Retarders go down and then up as wheels roll over them. If the wagon is travelling too fast, a piston inside the retarder stops it being pressed down so quickly. As the retarder resists the wheels, it slows the wagon down.

A French kangaroo

Lorry with container load.

Wheeled container rolls down into pouch.

This picture shows a French container system. French railways have a lower loading gauge than other railways. This means the distance from the wagon floor to the ground is smaller, so containers can be loaded onto the wagons by a lorry. Each wagon has a kangaroo-style pouch. As you can see in the picture, the container's wheels drop neatly into the pouch, which hangs underneath the wagon. The bottom of the container then rests firmly on the wagon floor.

A hydrocracker reactor of 558 tonnes (549.2 tons) holds the record for the heaviest freight ever carried on rails.

Giants on rails

The largest and heaviest steam engines were the 4-8-8-4 Big Boys, built for the Union Pacific Railroad from 1941 to 1944 in the USA.

The Big Boys were articulated, with a front set of wheels that swivelled when going around bends. A huge Russian locomotive, with an unarticulated rigid frame, was so restricted around bends, it had to be taken out of service.

To get round sharp bends, Big Boys had a leading set of eight driving wheels pivoted under the boiler, and a four-wheel swivelling bogie at the front.

Giant truck chains

Big Boys hauled long loads over the 1 in 67 gradient found in parts of the Wasatch Mountains in the USA. The train here has 70 trucks.

Garratts, like the Australian one shown below, were also giant articulated locomotives. They had one boiler in the middle, with sets of driving wheels at each end. The biggest Garratt ever was built in England in 1932 for the USSR railways. It was 5.2 m (17 ft) high.

Big Boys were 3.4 m (11 ft) wide and 4.9 m (16 ft) high. They were 39.9 m (131 ft) long, and with their tenders (not shown here) they weighed 508 tonnes (500 tons).

The rear set of eight driving wheels was fixed to the frame. Steam for the pistons and cylinders of all the driving wheels came from one gigantic boiler.

The firebox grate had an area of almost 14 square metres (151 sq ft). It could burn 22 tonnes (21.7 tons) of coal an hour. Mechanical stokers had to be used.

Mechanical stokers are usually Archimedes' screws - spiral screws of metal inside a hollow tube. As the screw turns, coal is drawn up around the thread.

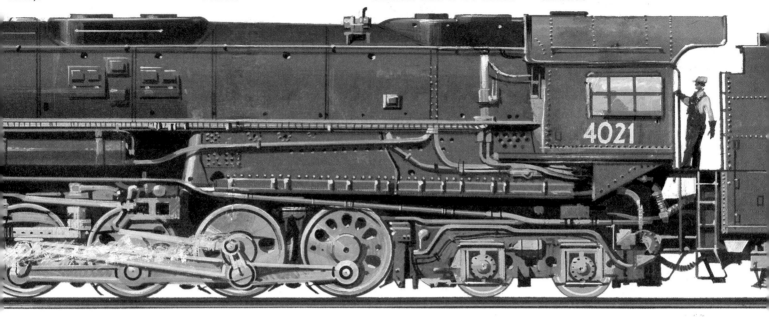

Heavyweight trains on lightweight tracks

Giant locomotives like the Big Boys were so heavy there was a danger of the track collapsing. Engineers increased the length of these locomotives to spread their load and so reduce strain on the track.

The experiment here will show you the effect of spreading load on track. You will need a piece of paper (about 290 x 210 mm or 11 x 8 in in size), four drinking straws, scissors, glue, stiff cardboard, and a pile of books.

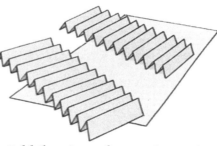

Fold the piece of paper into a zig-zag concertina. 15-20 folds will do. Try and get the folds as even as possible. Close the concertina up tightly and cut in half, to make two concertinas. These will be the track base that supports the rails.

Glue the straws lengthways on the concertinas, as shown above. These will be the rails and it is important that they each have the same gauge. About 5 cm (2 in) apart is the best gauge. Put the track to one side and leave to dry.

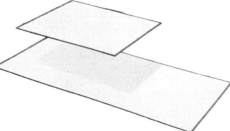

Cut two rectangles of cardboard to represent a long and short load. One must be 9 cm (3½ in) long and 6 cm (2½ in) wide. The second must be 18 cm (7 in) long and 9 cm (3½ in) wide and will represent the long wheelbase of the Big Boy engine.

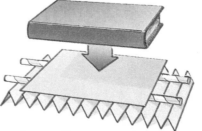

Lay the smaller rectangle across one set of concertina track. Gently start loading books onto it until the track collapses. In our tests the track collapsed under a weight of 1.9 kg (4 lbs 3 oz). Check and record your own "collapse weight".

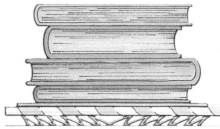

Now do the same with the second set of track and the longer rectangle. It should take the "collapse weight" of the smaller rectangle easily. Add more books until this track also collapses. Our "Big Boy" prototype collapsed at 4 kg (8 lb 13 oz).

The longest ever train pulled 500 wagons of coal in the USA. It was about 6.5 km (4 miles) long.

Strange trains

Railway engineers have come up with some amazing ideas. But their strange inventions were not always successful, and sometimes more of a fantastic experiment than a useful, working locomotive.

To make trains faster and to lay track more cheaply, these are the main problems facing engineers, who often found some weird solutions.

Some of the inventions create problems themselves, like the double-funnel train which needed mobile steps to help passengers across the track. Others flopped badly when unforeseen problems arose, like the British Advanced Passenger Train (APT). It took corners at top speed by tilting. This worked well, except that passengers always felt sick.

The underwater railway

Nicknamed Daddy Longlegs, this electric train, with 7 m (23 ft) high legs, ran on a 4.4 km (2.7 mile) track at Brighton Beach. Storms damaged the rails so it closed after five years.

The giant-wheeled train ▲

This Crampton-type Norris engine ran in the USA during the 1850s. Pistons turn big wheels as quickly as small ones, but one turn of a big wheel drives a train further than one turn of a small wheel. This is how large driving wheels achieved high speeds. Top speed was 110 km/h (68.4 mph).

The camelback train ▲

Camelbacks earned their name from the position of the driver's cab which lay over the top of the boiler. The fireman stood on a platform at the back. The firebox was wide with a large grate to burn slack coal. This 1854 camelback ran for almost 50 years on America's Baltimore and Ohio Railroad. It had six driving wheels and a four-wheel swivelling bogie.

The largest railway waiting rooms in the world are at Beijing in China.

The vacuum-tube train

The vacuum-tube train ran in south-west England in the 1840s. It did not have locomotives hauling the carriages. Instead it was powered by a series of pumps, which sucked air out of a vacuum tube that lay between the rails. Air pressure behind the piston pushed it into the vacuum. The train was attached to the piston and drawn with it along the rails. But rats ate the leather flaps which sealed the tube. This meant air leaked, the vacuum was lost and the train ground to a halt.

Driver

Vacuum tube

Piston

The propeller-driven ▲ train

The Kruckenburg (above) was a German single-car train which broke the world record in 1931 when it maintained a speed of 230 km/h (142.9 mph) for a distance of 10 km (6.2 miles). Its propeller was powered by a Maybach diesel engine used in Zeppelin airships. The train was built as an experiment to test stability and streamlining at high speeds.

The double-funnel ▶ train

This locomotive (right) was invented by Charles Lartigue, a Frenchman, and ran on the Listowel and Ballybunion Railway in Ireland, from 1888 to 1924. It had twin boilers and ran on top of an A-shaped track that could be laid cheaply and quickly.

There were supports either side of the track to stop it tipping over and loads had to be balanced.

In London in 1891, the Great Eastern Railway assembled a locomotive in a record time of 9 hours, 57 minutes.

Superspeed trains

Modern high-speed trains are some of the most exciting in the world today. France, Germany, Britain and Japan are all developing new technology to make their railways faster and more competitive. Modern motorways and jetplanes mean that passengers can travel quickly and comfortably to their destination. So, to compete successfully the latest long-distance trains must have high speeds and provide a relaxing and comfortable journey. The importance of speed was understood from the time of Rocket, which won the world record at 46.8 km/h (29.1 mph) in 1829. But 161 years later, in 1990 the French TGV raced down its specially built track in a test run, achieving a record-shattering speed of 515.3 km/h (320.2 mph). The Japanese Maglev Linear Express may reach 600 km/h (373 mph) by the beginning of the 21st century - Thirteen times faster than the Rocket.

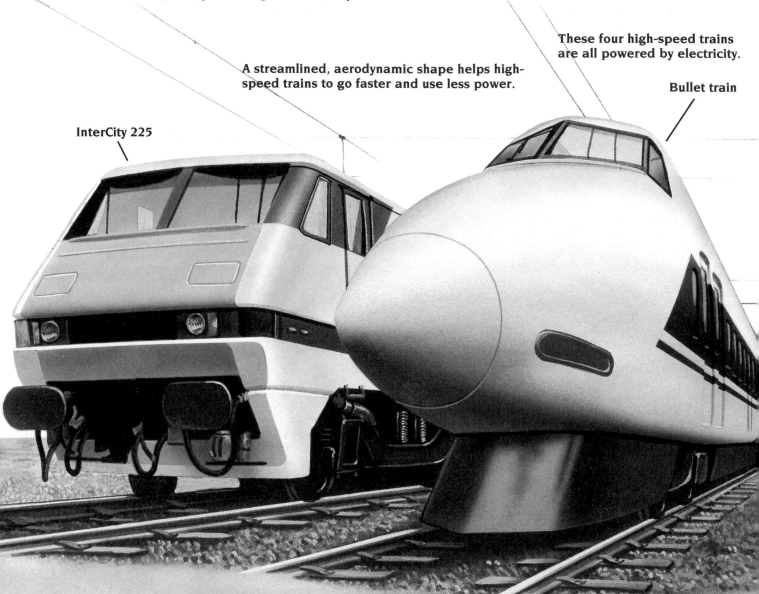

These four high-speed trains are all powered by electricity.

Bullet train

A streamlined, aerodynamic shape helps high-speed trains to go faster and use less power.

InterCity 225

InterCity 225 (Britain)

The InterCity 225 has Britain's most powerful ever locomotive, a Class 91 electric designed to run at a maximum speed of 225 km/h (139.8 mph). The Class 91 is at one end of the train and a Driving Van Trailer (DVT) at the other end. When the DVT is leading, the driver controls the Class 91 from the DVT. New technology means the driver can select a speed and the Class 91 will accelerate to it under computer control, saving energy and giving a smoother ride.

Bullet train (Japan)

The famous electric Bullet train is a gleaming, stream-lined train that travels at top speeds of 220 km/h (136.7 mph). A speed of 319 km/h (198.2mph) has been recorded on test track. The train runs on the Shinkansen line from Tokyo to many other Japanese cities and carries thousands of passengers each day. The record for passengers carried on one day was 807,875 in 1975, and over 300 million people were carried in the ten years from 1980 to 1990.

The world speed record for diesel traction was set in 1987 when a British prototype reached 283.4 km/h (176 mp

TGV (France)

The French TGV (Train à Grande Vitesse, which means "high-speed train") is the world speed record holder at 515.3 km/h (320.2 mph), and has an average speed of about 300 km/h (186.4 mph). A streamlined, electric train, the TGV has a network of routes covering much of France. It even reaches into Switzerland. At low speeds the TGV travels on normal railway lines, but at high speeds switches to specially designed and built track. The trains have a locomotive at either end, and power is transmitted to the engine by pantographs picking up electric current from overhead wires. Computers play a large part in the running of the train. High-power brakes work with a computer controlled anti-lock system for each axle, and the driver has a computer screen in his cab to warn him of technical problems. He is also linked by radio with the signalling and control post in Paris, which controls all TGV traffic.

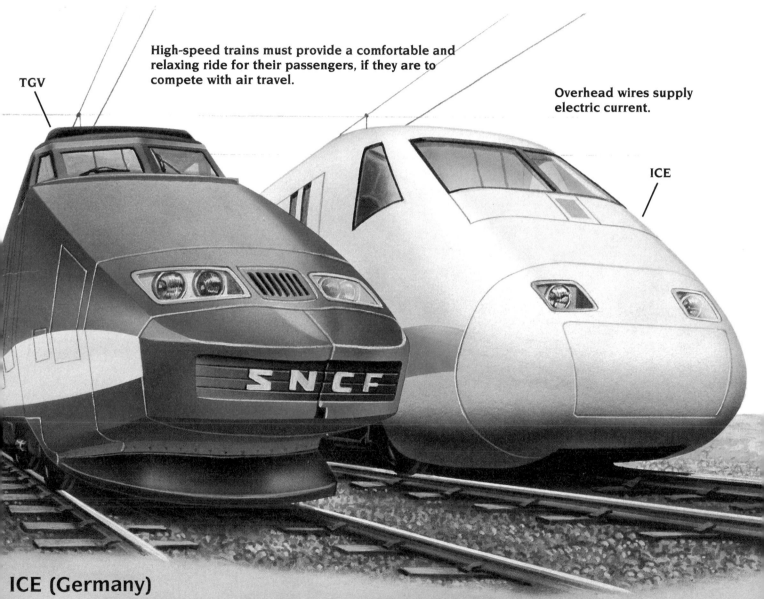

High-speed trains must provide a comfortable and relaxing ride for their passengers, if they are to compete with air travel.

TGV

Overhead wires supply electric current.

ICE

ICE (Germany)

The new German ICE (InterCity Express) has already been tested at more than 400 km/h (248.6 mph), and when it goes into service in 1992 will run at up to 250 km/h (155.3 mph). There are two locomotives at either end of the train, and pantographs send electric current to the engine. Like all high-speed trains it has good aerodynamics with a sleek, streamlined shape. With fast journeys and a high level of comfort, it is expected that the ICE will steal passengers from airlines flying between German cities. There are many luxuries on board like phones and lounges, and attached to each seat is a system which provides travel information and entertainment. From 1993 ICE carriages will be designed for use in France and other parts of Europe. This means that passengers will be able to travel in one high-speed train across many different countries.

In France in 1971, L'Aérotrain, reached a speed of 427 km/h (265 mph)

Rail records

From 1829 to 1990 the world railway speed record rose from 46.8 km/h to 515.3 km/h (29.1 mph to 320.2 mph). Speed is practical as well as exciting. Every extra 2 km/h (1.2 miles) in speed can bring a 1% increase in passengers.

High-speed rail travel is very safe compared with roads. On the New South Wales railway system in Australia, from 1963 to 1977, there were no deaths at all, while road deaths were in the thousands.

The world slow-speed rail record must be held by a train from Texas. In mid journey, the track was washed away, stranding the train. Seven years later new track was built and the train finally reached its destination.

Speed records

Rocket, England, 1829	Steam		
Great Britain, England, 1848	Steam		
999, USA, 1893	Steam		
Siemens & Halske, Germany, 1903	Electric		
Borsig, 05.001, Germany, 1935	Steam		
CC 7107, France, 1955	Electric		
ICE, Germany, 1988	Electric		
TGV, France, 1990	Electric		

0   50

The fastest thing on rails

In 1959 this rocket-powered sled zoomed along the Supersonic Naval Ordnance Research Track (SNORT) in New Mexico, USA. It reached an amazing 4,972 km/h (3,090 mph) during high speed tests. Instead of rolling on wheels, like normal locomotives, it slid along on metal shoes. The shoes fitted snugly into slots on the rails to keep it on the track. The nose-section was taken from a B58 Hustler aircraft.

Most luxurious train

In 1883 a train steamed away from Paris bound for distant Romania. It had two luxurious sleeping cars, a dining car and a smoking lounge. When it reached its destination King Charles of Romania entertained the passengers. This was the first journey of the Orient Express.

Today the train is as luxurious as ever, running between London and Venice with stops in Paris, Zurich, Innsbruck and Salzburg. There are 11 sleeping cars and three restaurant cars. Passengers can even listen to live music in the piano bar.

Each cabin has hot water, a bed, special soap and writing paper.

The longest railway in the world

The Trans-Siberian Railway was completed in 1916 and stretches 9,297 km (5,777 miles) from Moscow to Vladivostok. The entire journey takes seven days and two hours.

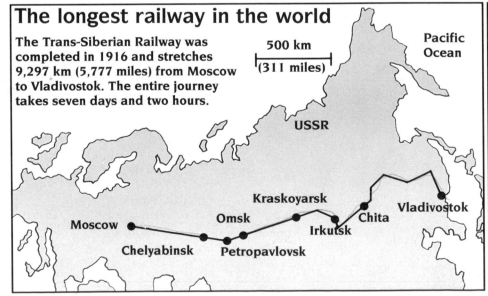

500 km
(311 miles)

Pacific Ocean

USSR

Moscow — Chelyabinsk — Petropavlovsk — Omsk — Kraskoyarsk — Irkutsk — Chita — Vladivostok

The longest straight

AUSTRALIA

Brisbane
Nullarbor Plain
Adelaide
Perth
Melbourne
Sydney

The Trans-Australian Railway includes the longest section of straight track in the world. This 478 km (297 miles) of standard gauge straight track crosses part of the treeless Nullarbor Plain.

The longest railway bridge in the world is the Huey P. Long in New Orleans, USA. It stretches 7,082 m (23,235 ft)

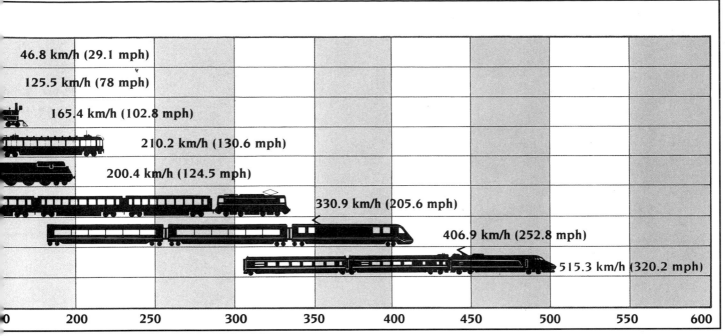

46.8 km/h (29.1 mph)

125.5 km/h (78 mph)

165.4 km/h (102.8 mph)

210.2 km/h (130.6 mph)

200.4 km/h (124.5 mph)

330.9 km/h (205.6 mph)

406.9 km/h (252.8 mph)

515.3 km/h (320.2 mph)

| 0 | 200 | 250 | 300 | 350 | 400 | 450 | 500 | 550 | 600 |

The most powerful diesel

The American Centennial is the world's most powerful diesel-electric locomotive. They were given this name because they were introduced in 1969, a century after the first transcontinental railway in the USA opened. They haul freight along the same route as the Big Boys did, and have a top speed of 115 km/h (71.5 mph). The Centennials are 29.3 m (96.1 ft) long and weigh 229 tonnes (225 tons).

The longest and the deepest railway tunnel

The Seikan tunnel in Japan is the longest in the world at 53.8 km (33.4 miles). It runs under the sea at a depth of 100 m (328 ft) below the seabed, and joins the islands of Honshu and Hokkaido, which are divided by the Tsugaru Straits. The straits can be very dangerous and ferries have sunk in typhoons. High-speed trains run through the tunnel.

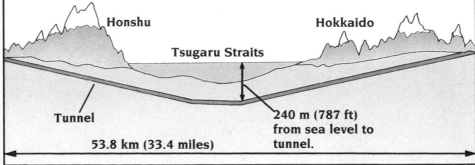

Honshu

Hokkaido

Tsugaru Straits

Tunnel

240 m (787 ft) from sea level to tunnel.

53.8 km (33.4 miles)

A station in Wales has the world's longest name - Llanfairpwllgwyngyllgogerychwyrndrobwllllantysiliogogogoch. 31

Index

Books

Trains are very popular, so you will always find interesting books on railway history and modern railways in bookshops. Here are a few of the many books you will be able to find.

The Guinness Railway Book John Marshall (Guinness Publishing)

Motive Power Recognition: 1 Locomotives Colin J. Marsden (Ian Allen)

Railway World Yearbook Colin Boocock (Ian Allen)

Day in the Life of British Rail Murray Brown (David and Charles)

25 Years of Railway Research Colin J. Marsden (OPC)

The Story of Trains. This is in the Discoverers' series. (Moonlight)

Model Railways

Model railways are a fascinating hobby. Here are some of the most popular you can buy.

Fleischmann make what are regarded as the finest model trains in the world.

Less expensive, and good value are Hornby, Dapol, Bachmann and Replica.